S Bradley

Y0-DKD-208

LADYBIRD BOOKS, INC.
Auburn, Maine 04210 U.S.A.
© LADYBIRD BOOKS LTD MCMLXXXVIII
Loughborough, Leicestershire, England

All rights reserved. No part of this publication may be reproduced, stored in a retrieval system, or transmitted in any form or by any means, electronic, mechanical, photocopying, recording or otherwise, without the prior consent of the copyright owner.

Printed in England

Baby Zoo Animals

by RONNE PELTZMAN RANDALL
illustrated by DAWN HOLMES

Ladybird Books

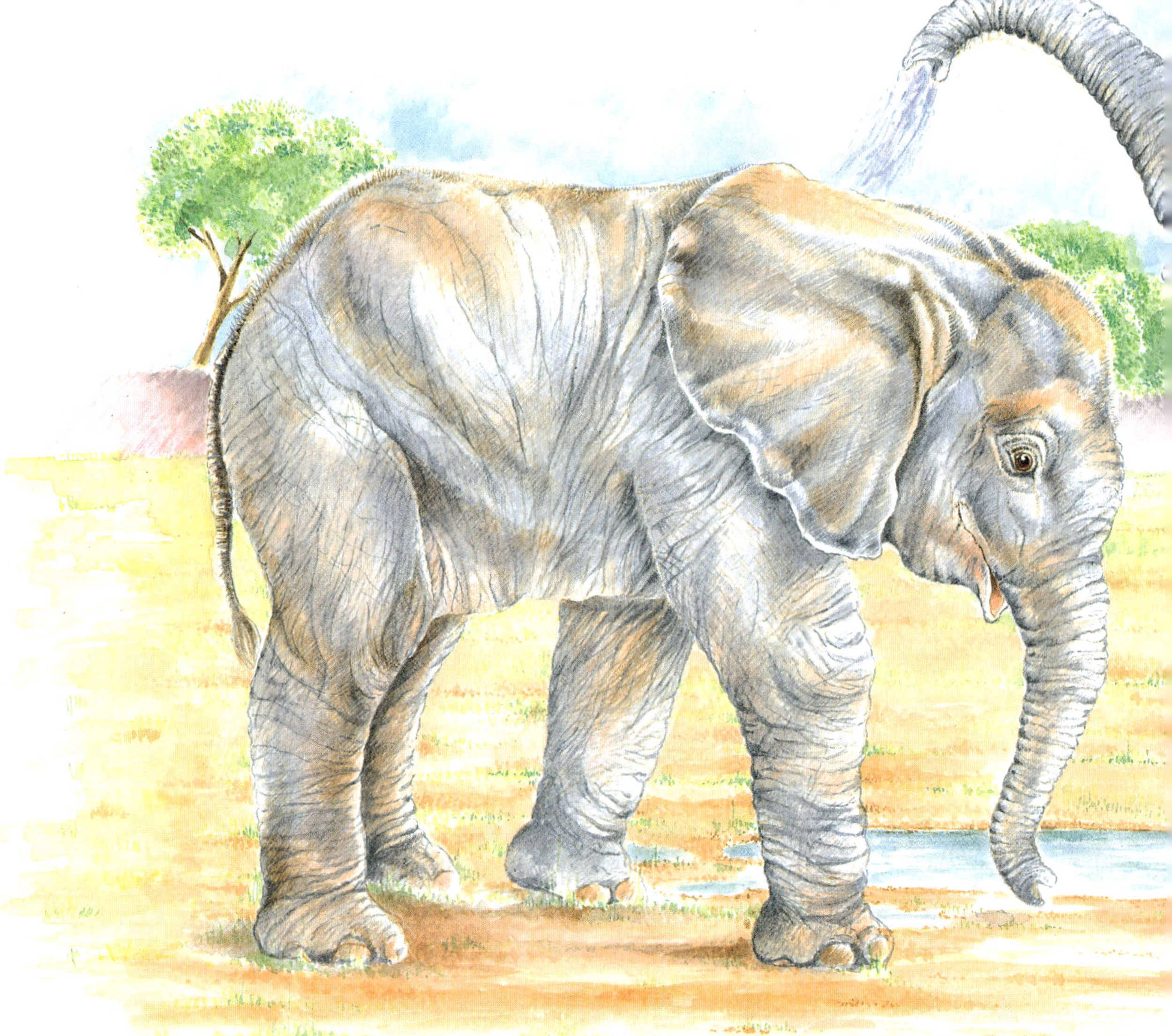

Baby elephant gives her brother a nice cool shower.

One baby giraffe reaches down
for some grass to eat.
Another reaches up
for some tasty green leaves.

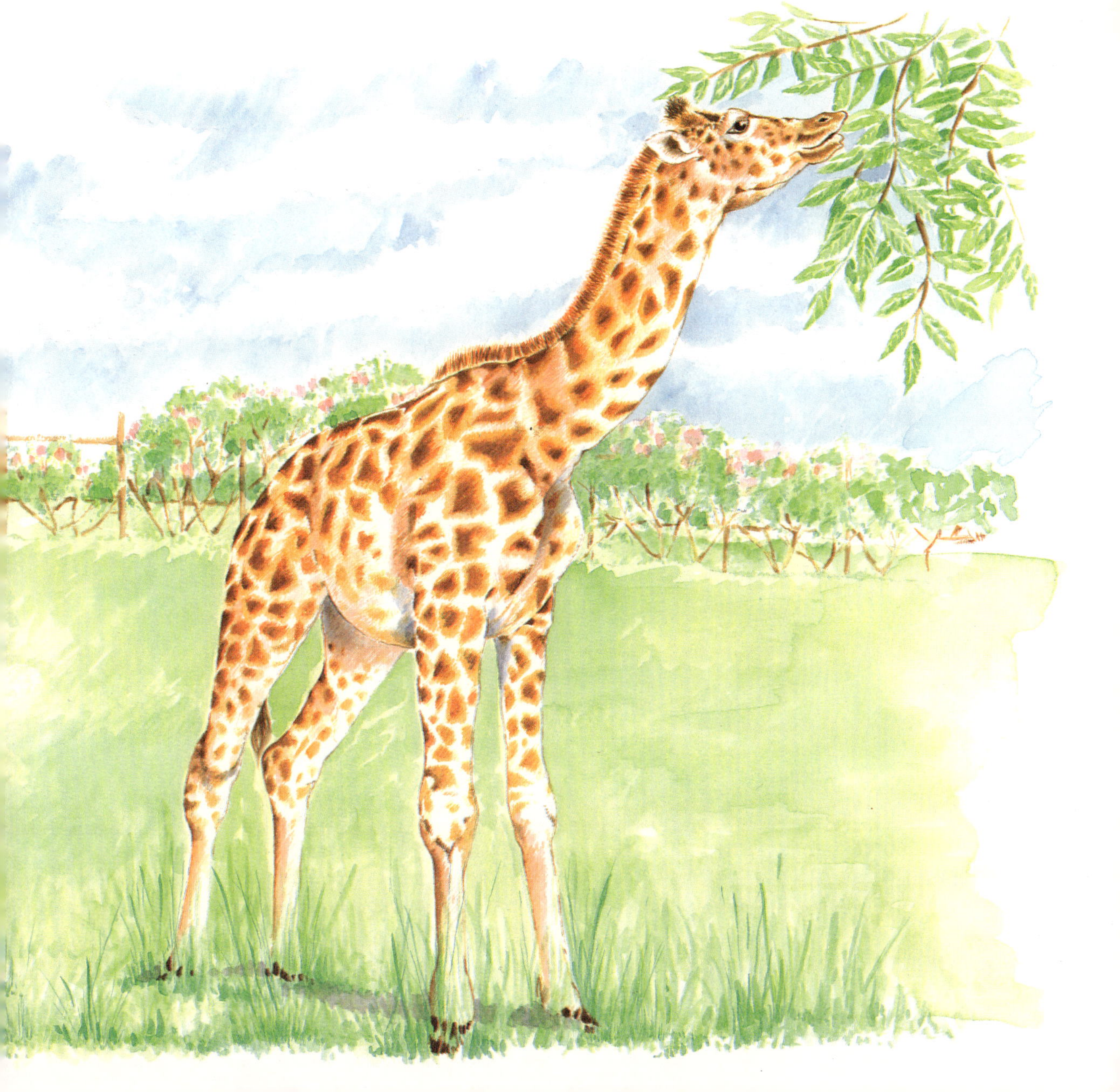

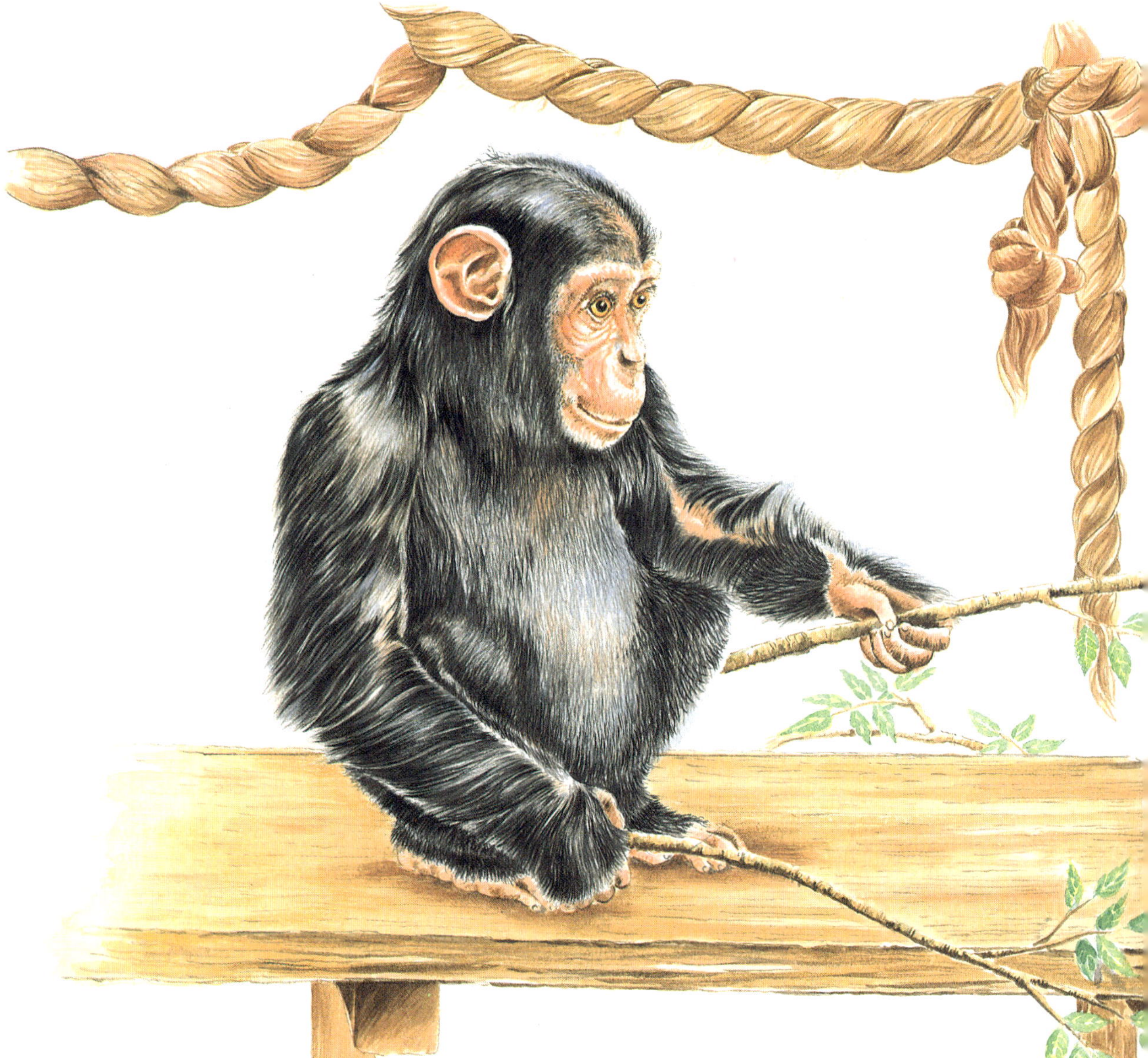

The baby chimpanzees like to climb high.

The baby zebras
have been taking a rest.
Now they're ready for a romp.

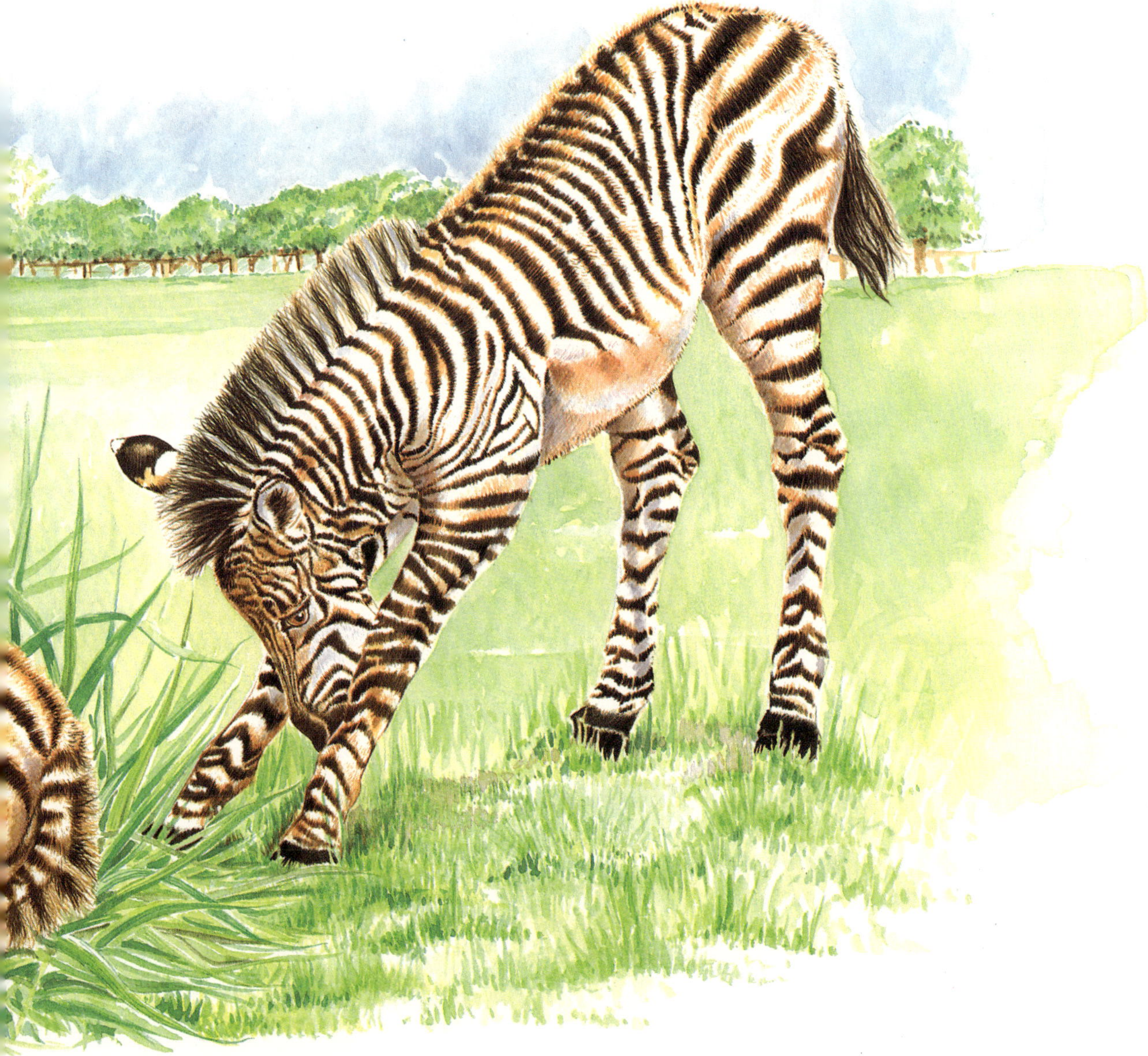

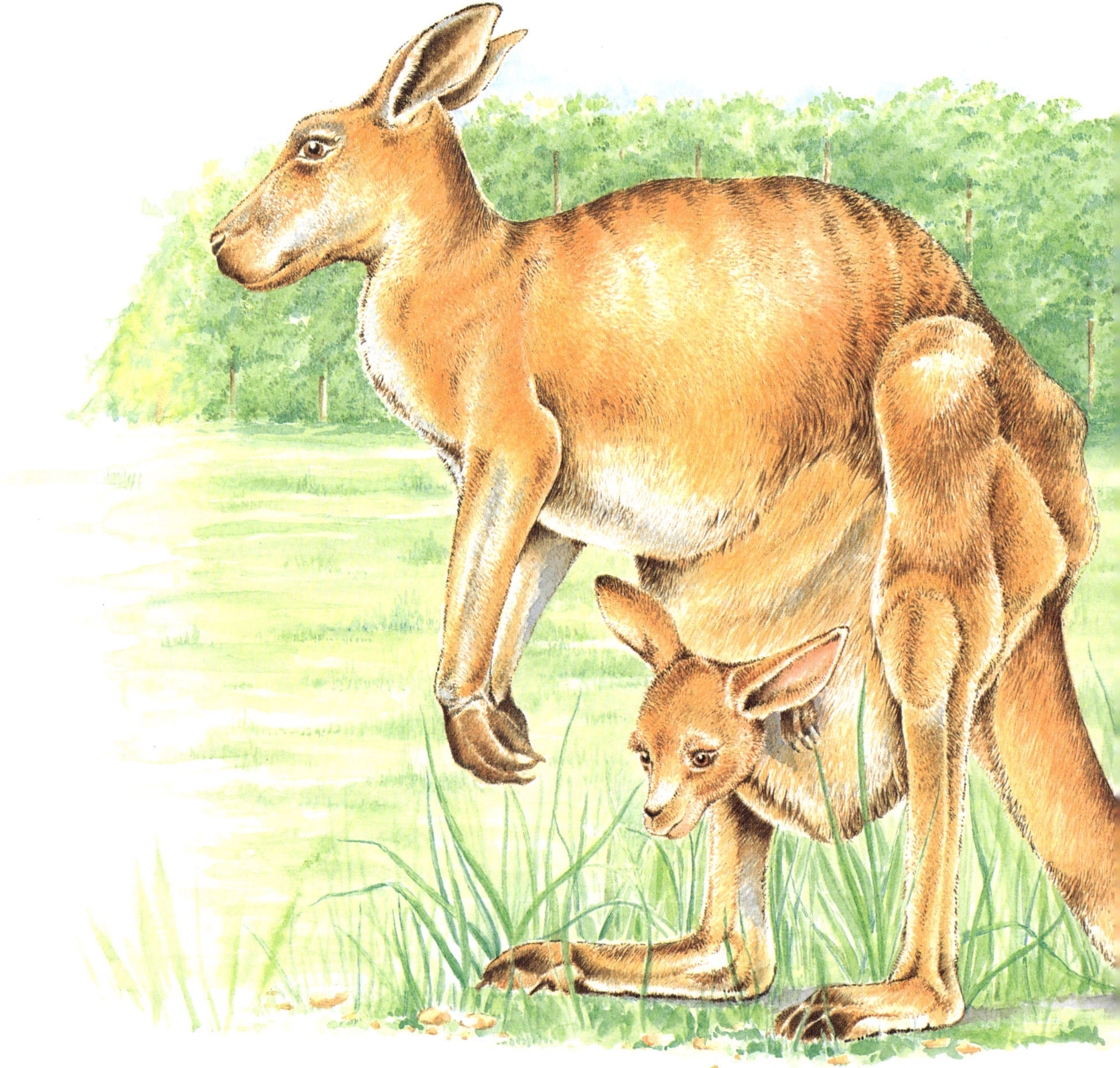

Baby kangaroo stays safe and snug in his mother's pouch.

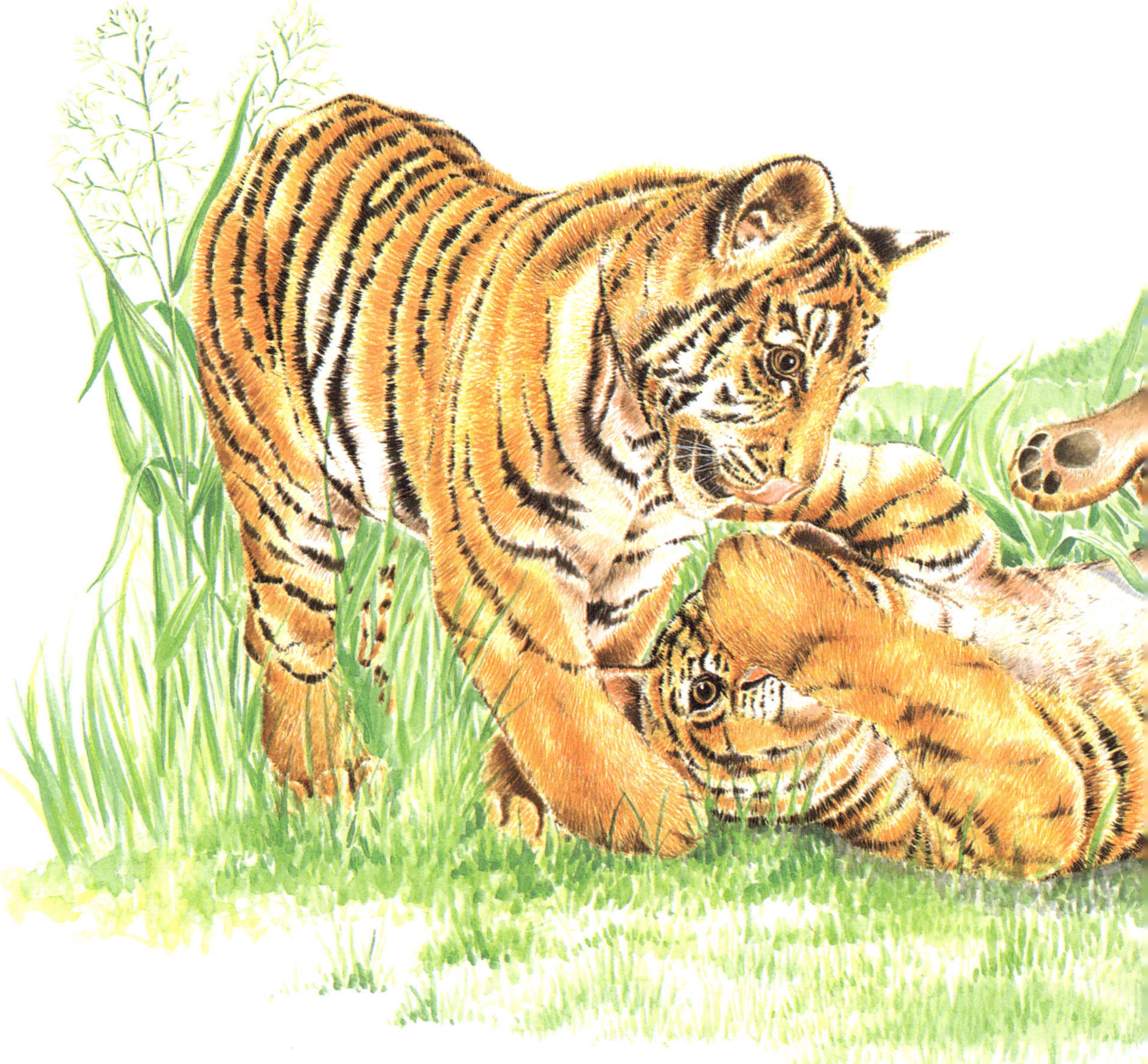

The frisky baby tigers
roll and wrestle and play...

...but the lion cubs
are feeling lazy today.

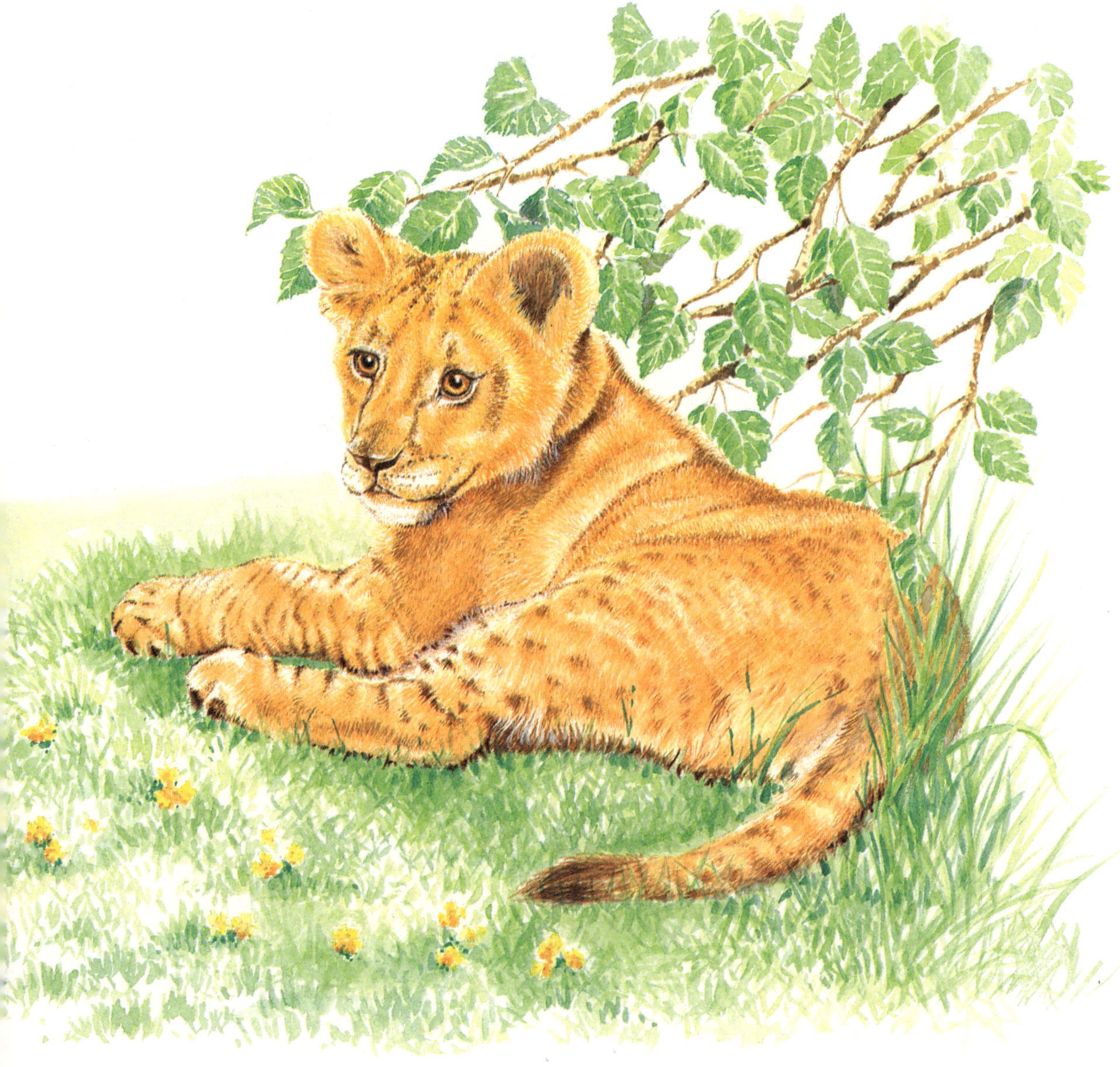

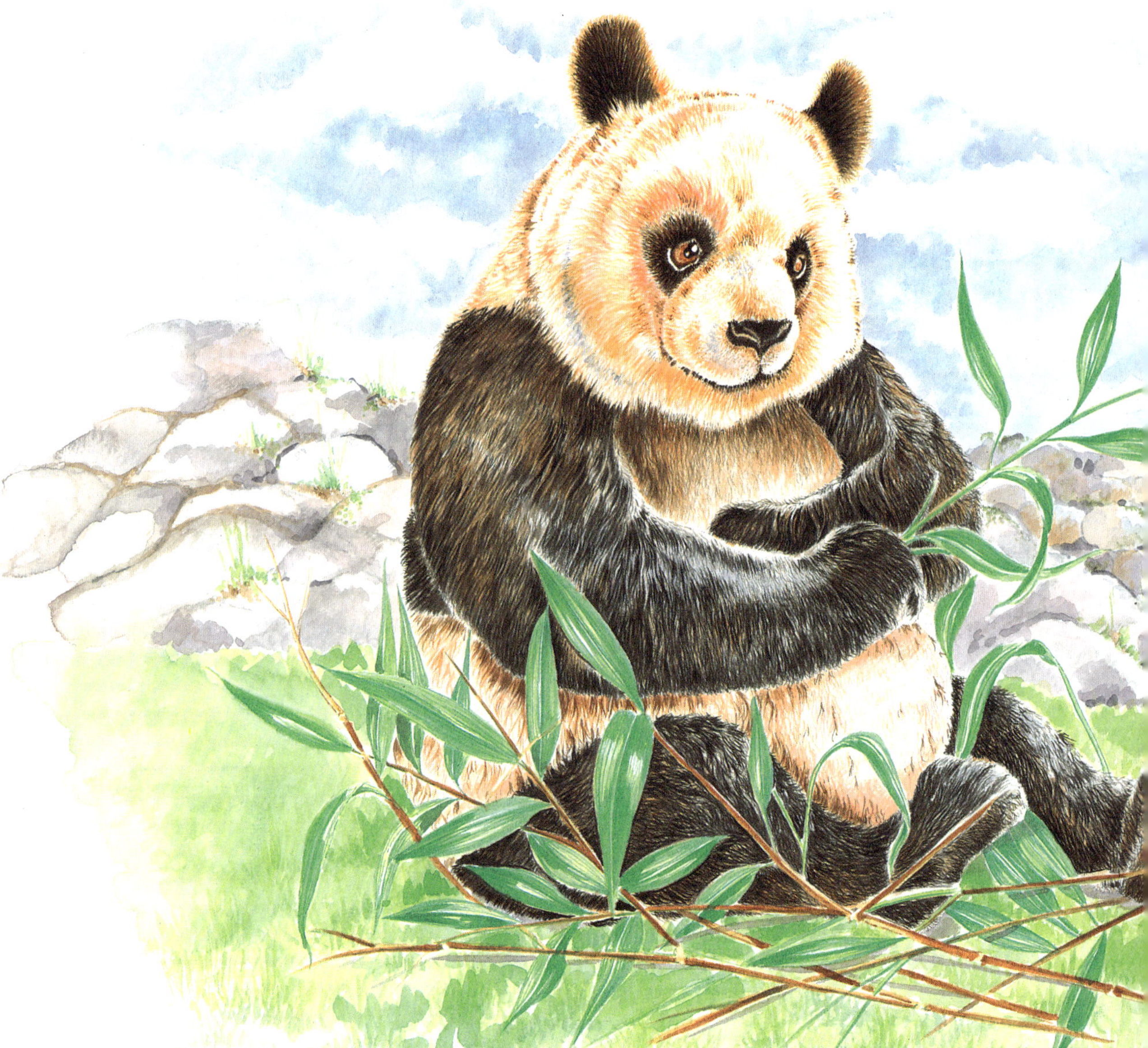

Baby panda and her mother love to eat bamboo leaves.

Baby camel has long, long legs.

Baby koala gets a ride on his mother's back.

The polar bear cubs stay cool in their icy pool.

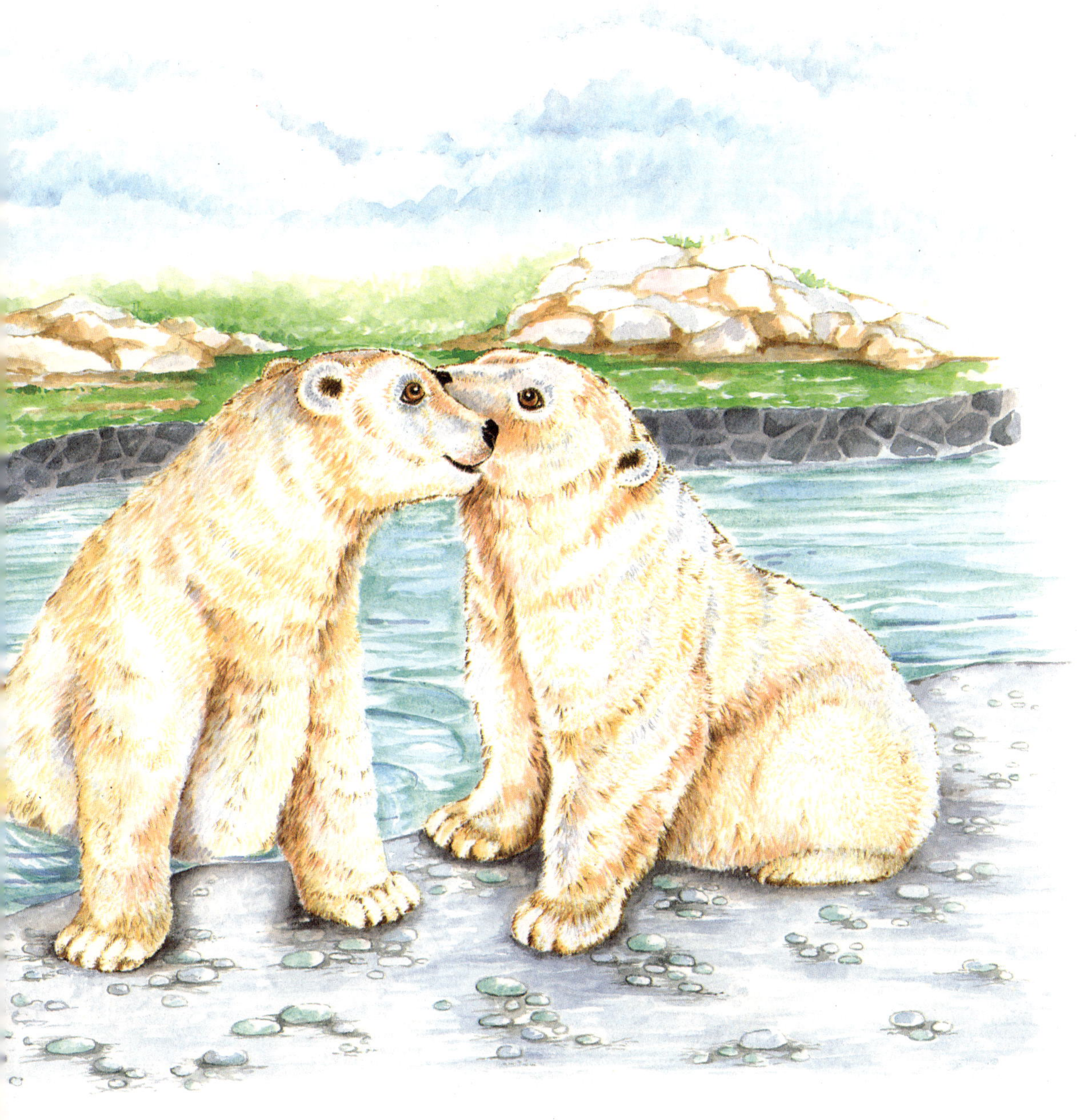

The baby hippos have fun wading with their mother.

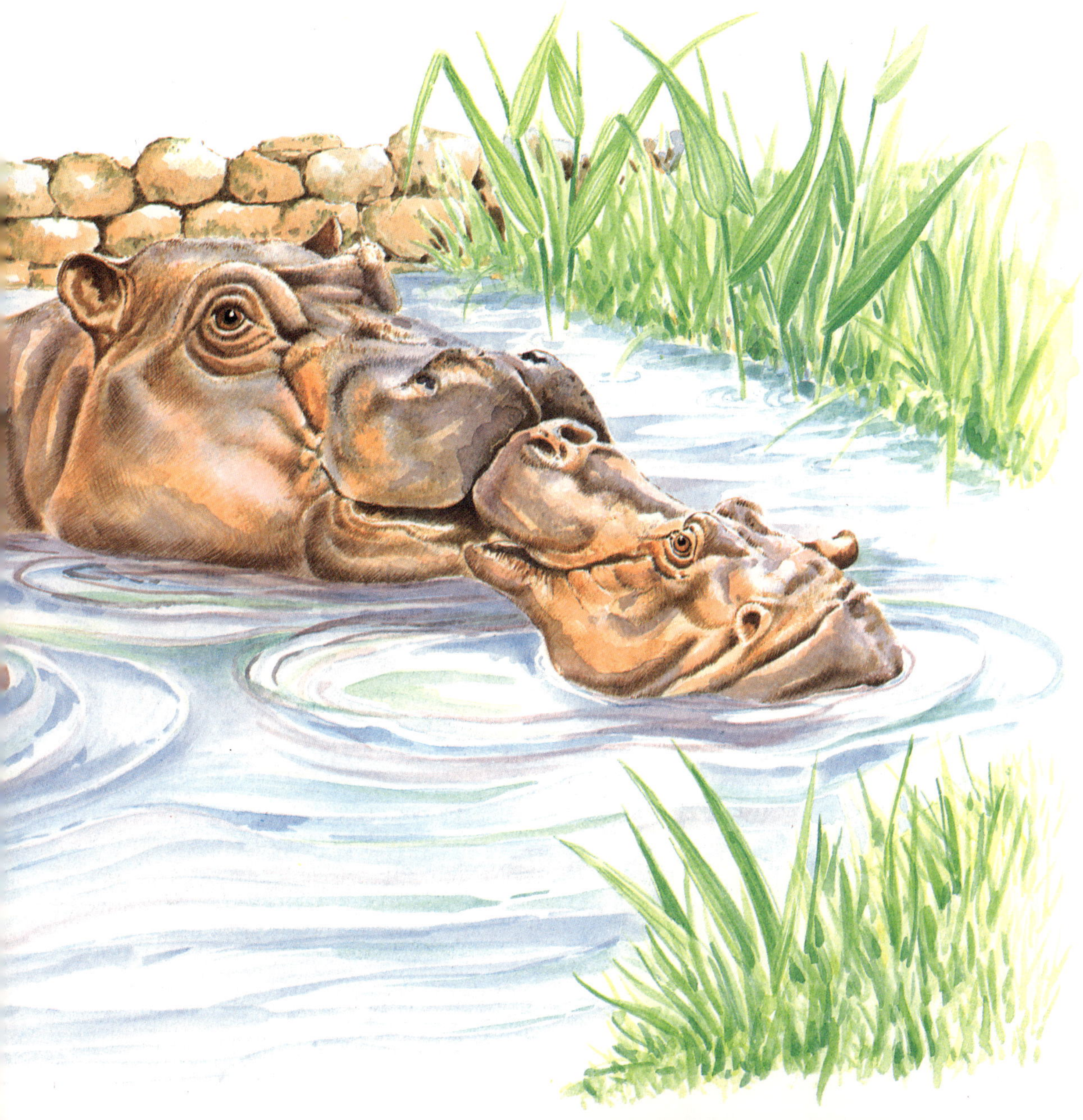

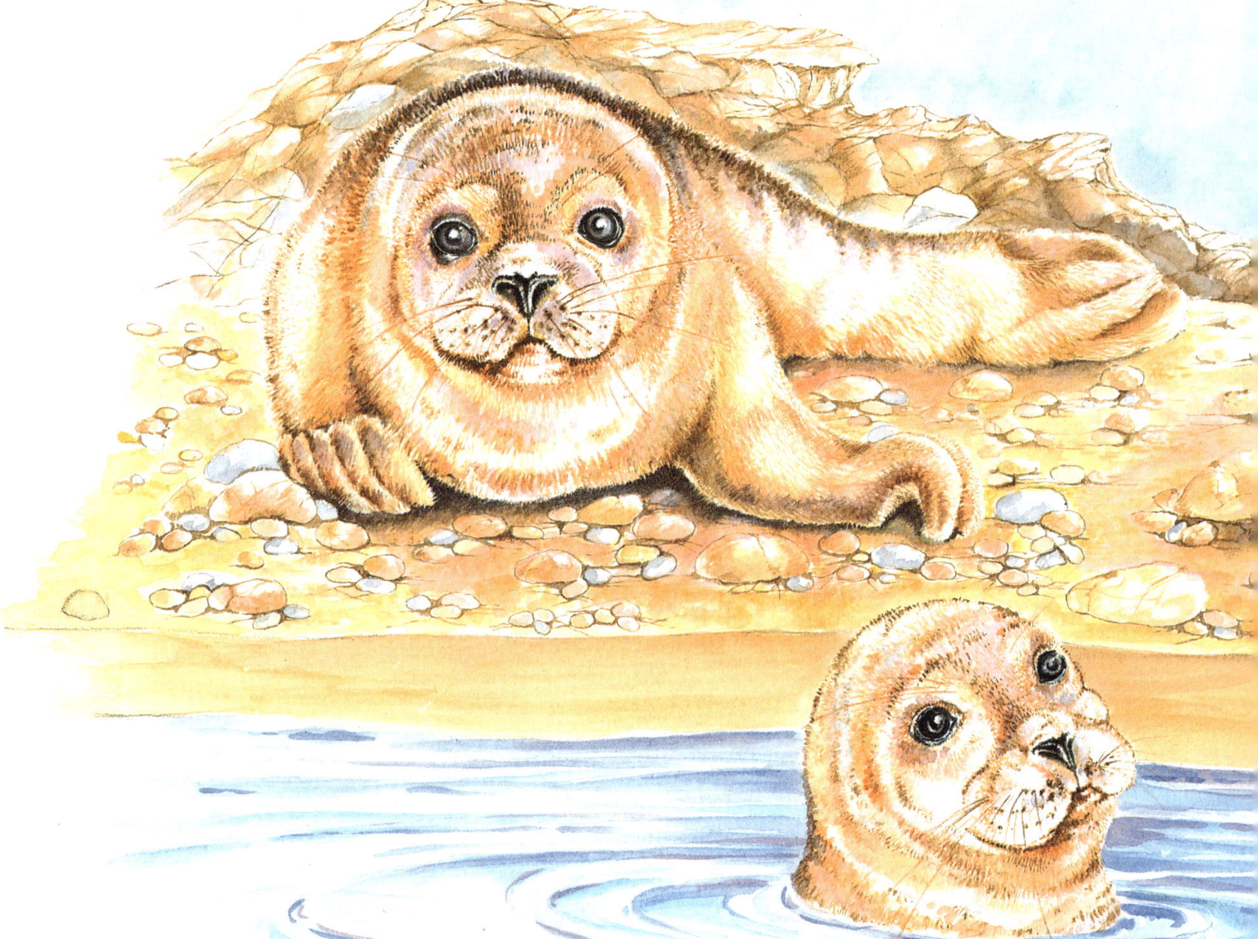

After a swim,
the baby seals like to stretch out
on the sunny rocks.

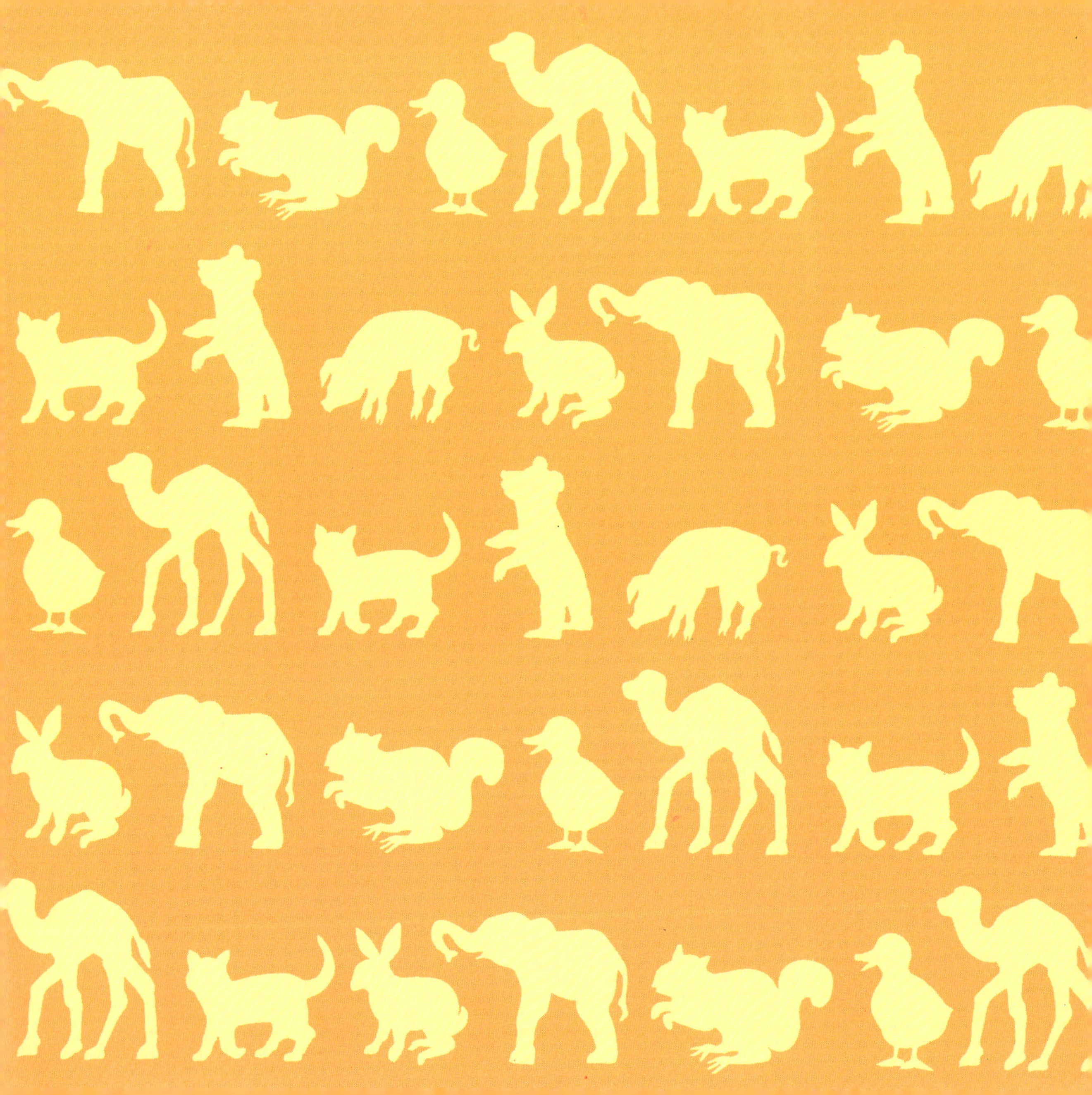